Life Cycle of a

Silkworm

Ron Fridell
and
Patricia Walsh

Heinemann Library
Chicago, Illinois

Designed by Wilkinson Design
Illustrated by David Westerfield
Printed by South China Printing Company, Hong Kong

05 04 03 02 01
10 9 8 7 6 5 4 3 2

Library of Congress Cataloging-in-Publication Data
Fridell, Ron.
    Life cycle of a silkworm / Ron Fridell, Patricia Walsh.
        p. cm.
Includes bibliographical references and index.
    ISBN 1-58810-094-4 (lib. bdg.)   ISBN 1-58810-396-X (pbk. bdg.)
    1. Silkworms—Life cycles—Juvenile literature. [1. Silkworms.] I.
Title: Silkworm. II. Walsh, Patricia, 1951- III. Title.
    SF542.5 .F75 2001
        638.2—dc21
                                                    00-011235

Acknowledgments
The Publisher would like to thank the following for permission to reproduce photographs:
Em Ahart pp.12, 21; Black Star Publishing/Scott Rutherford/PictureQuest p.25; Bruce Coleman Inc./E. R. Degginger pp.7, 13, 26/Picturequest, /Pam Taylor p.10; Corbis/Gallo Images /Anthony Bannister pp.14, 15, 28, 29, /Wolfgang Kaehler p.24, /Charles and Josette Lenars p.23, /Stephanie Maze p.11, /Robert Pickett pp.20, 29; Dwight Kuhn pp.6, 8, 16, 19, 28; National Geographic Society/Stephanie Maze p.5; Photo Researchers Inc./S. Nagendra p.27; SPL/Photo Researchers Inc/Pascal Goetgheluck pp.16, 29; Stock, Boston/PictureQuest/Cary Wolinsky p.22; University of Nebraska/James Kalisch pp.4, 9, 17, 18, 29.

Cover photograph reproduced with the permission of Dwight Kuhn.

Special thanks to the University of Nebraska, Department of Entomology and Mr. James Kalisch.

Every effort has been made to contact copyright holders of any material reproduced in this book. Any omissions will be rectified in subsequent printings if notice is given to the Publisher.

Some words are shown in bold, **like this.** You can find out what they mean by looking in the glossary.

Contents

Meet the Silkworms

A silkworm is an **insect.** It is not a worm. It is a caterpillar. A silkworm looks like it has many legs, but only six are true legs. It uses the other ten legs to cling to plants.

1 day

3 weeks

5 weeks

Many years ago, silkworms lived in the wild. Today silkworms live only on silk farms. Silkworms are **domesticated.** Silk farmers **raise** them to get the silk thread used to make silk cloth.

10 weeks

11 weeks

Egg

The silkworm begins life in a tiny egg. The egg is one of about 300 sticky, yellow eggs laid by the female silk **moth.**

1 day

3 weeks

5 weeks

The egg needs to be cold for a few weeks. Then the egg is warmed up and its center turns black. The warm egg **hatches** in about ten days.

8 weeks

10 weeks

11 weeks

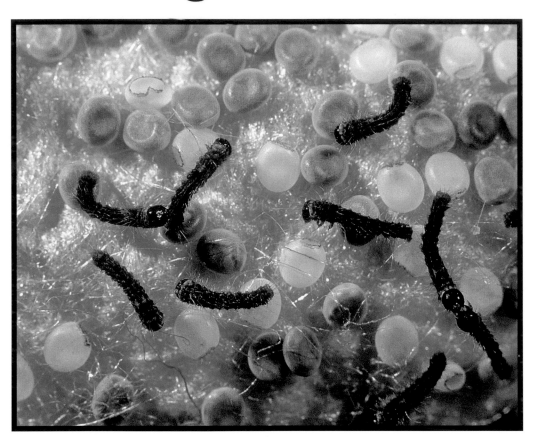

8

When the tiny silkworm **larva** is ready to **hatch,** it bites a hole in the egg. Then it wriggles out.

1 day

3 weeks

5 weeks

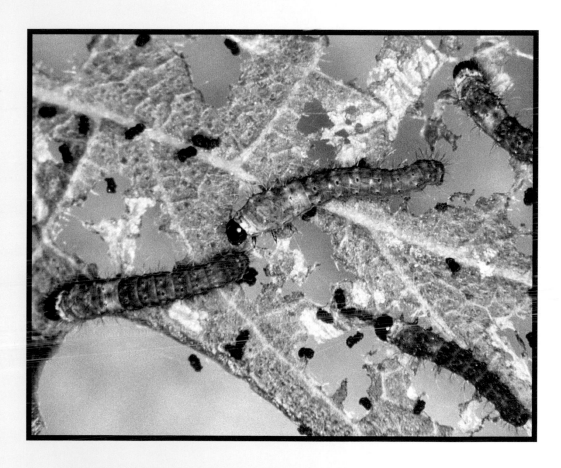

The newly hatched silkworm larva looks like a tiny black string. At first it is too weak to crawl very far, but it is ready to eat.

8 weeks

10 weeks

11 weeks

Larva

The new **larva** needs to have its food close by. It eats only mulberry tree leaves. In a few days, the larva will be stronger. It will crawl from leaf to leaf.

1 day

3 weeks

5 weeks

The larva eats a lot of mulberry leaves. It does not drink water. It gets enough **moisture** from the leaves.

8 weeks

10 weeks

11 weeks

Molting

12

The **larva's** skin does not stretch as it grows. To get bigger, a silkworm must **molt.** The old skin splits. The silkworm wriggles out wearing its new skin.

1 day

3 weeks

5 weeks

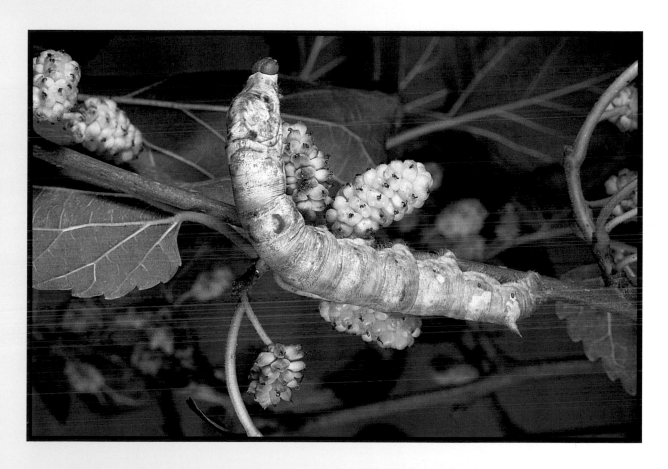

The larva molts four times. After the fourth molt, the larva eats even more mulberry leaves than it did before. It grows to be about as long as your finger.

8 weeks   10 weeks   11 weeks

Spinning the Cocoon 8 weeks

The **larva** is ready to spin a
cocoon. It makes its cocoon from
one long, sticky silk thread that
comes from its mouth.

1 day

3 weeks

5 weeks

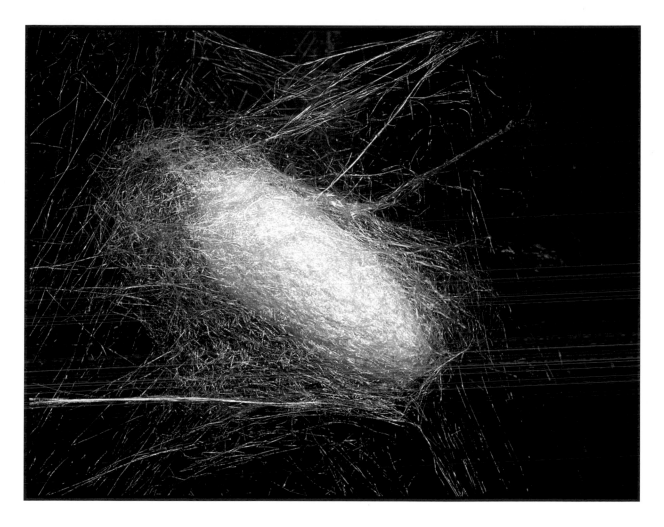

First the larva spins a silk web. Then it spins and spins for three days. It spins a silk cocoon around itself.

8 weeks

10 weeks

11 weeks

Pupa

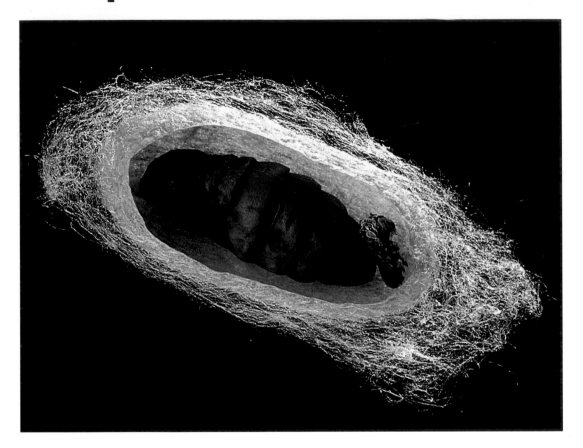

Inside the **cocoon,** the **larva molts** one last time. This time it changes to a brown **pupa** with a hard shell.

1 day

3 weeks

5 weeks

cocoon　　　　**moth**

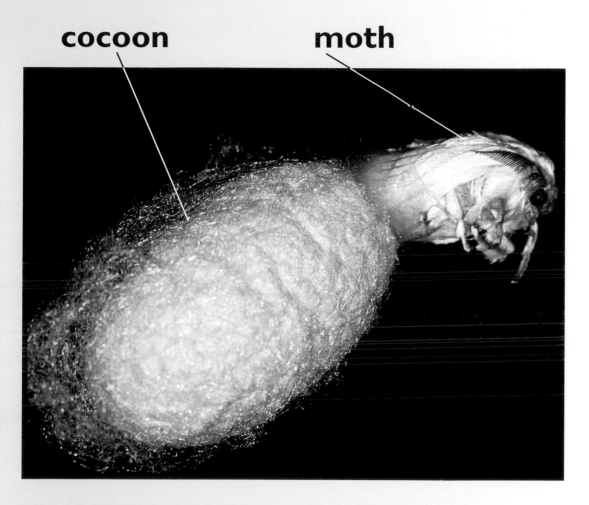

After two weeks, the shell splits.
The pupa has changed to a white
adult **moth**. It has wings, large
eyes, and feathery **antennae.**

8 weeks　　　　　10 weeks　　　　　11 weeks

Leaving the Cocoon 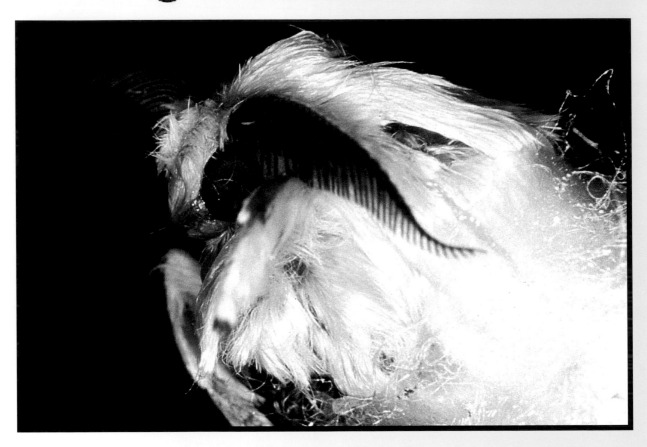10 weeks

It is time for the silk **moth** to leave the **cocoon.** To get out, it spits a special liquid. The liquid wets the inside of the cocoon and makes a hole in the strong silk.

1 day

3 weeks

5 weeks

The silk moth pulls itself through the hole. In about an hour, its damp wings unfold and dry.

8 weeks 10 weeks 11 weeks

Silk Moth

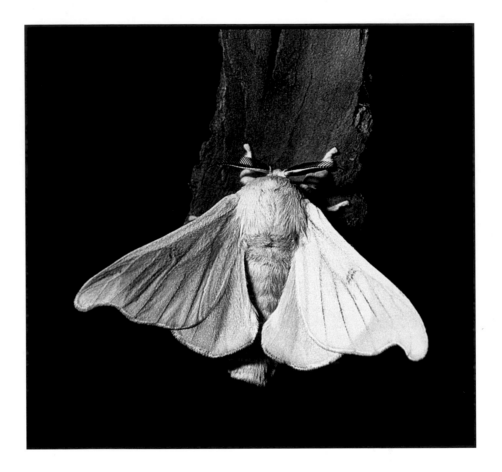

The silk **moth** has six legs and two **antennae.** It also has four wings, but it cannot fly. It only flutters and hops.

I day

3 weeks

5 weeks

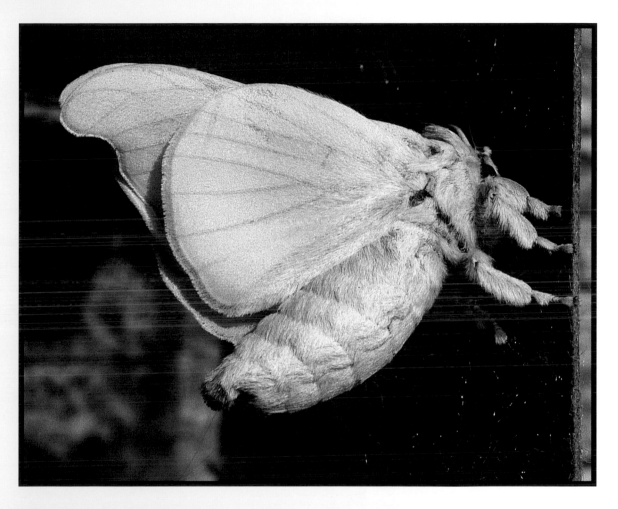

For the next few days, the silk moth does not eat or drink anything.

8 weeks

10 weeks

11 weeks

Silk from Silkworms

Silk farmers **raise** silkworms for their **cocoons.** The silk thread of the cocoons is woven into silk cloth.

I day

3 weeks

5 weeks

On silk farms, most **pupas** never change into **moths.** If moths were allowed to come out of the cocoons, there would be holes in the cocoons. They would be useless for making silk cloth.

8 weeks

10 weeks

11 weeks

Making Silk Cloth

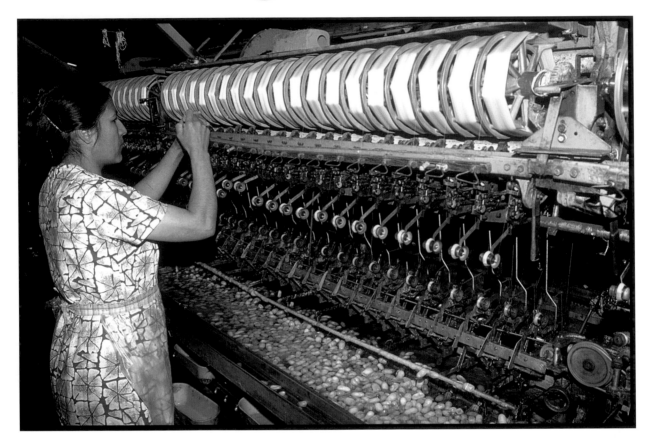

The long, white silk thread from the **cocoon** is as thin as a spiderweb. It is unwound from the cocoon. Machines twist the threads together to make one **strand** of silk.

1 day

3 weeks

5 weeks

The strands are woven into silk cloth. The cloth can be **dyed** any color to make beautiful clothing like this.

8 weeks

10 weeks

11 weeks

Mating

The female **moth** is bigger than the male. Soon after coming out of the **cocoon,** she gives off a **scent** to help the male find her. Then they **mate.**

1 day

3 weeks

5 weeks

After mating, the male moth dies. The female moth lays her eggs a few hours after mating. Then she will die, too.

8 weeks

10 weeks

11 weeks

Life Cycle

Egg

1

Larva

2

3

Larva

28

Cocoon

Pupa

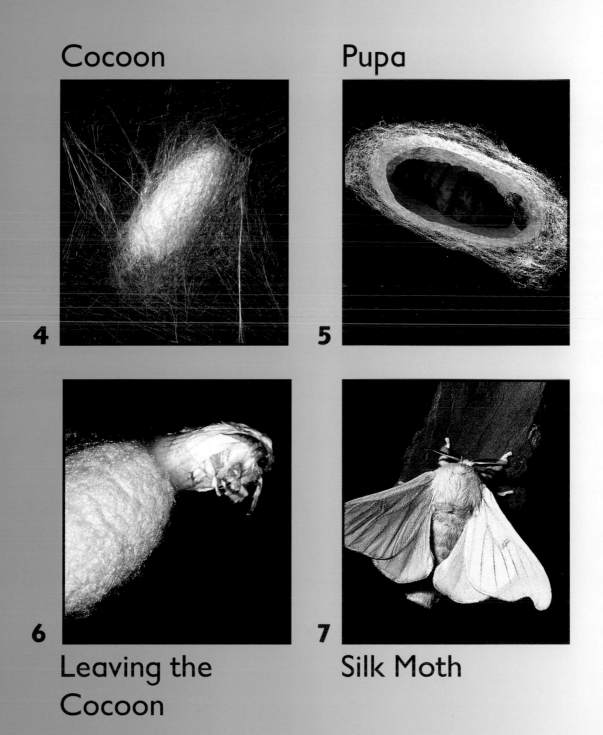

4

5

6

7

Leaving the Cocoon

Silk Moth

Fact File

The silkworm **larva** moves its head back and forth in a figure eight pattern as it spins its **cocoon.**

It takes 110 cocoons to make a silk tie. It takes 630 cocoons to make a silk shirt.

Other kinds of **moths** can fly to escape **predators,** but a silkworm moth has no predators and does not fly.

A single thread of silk from a cocoon can be as long as a mile. That is about as long as seventeen soccer fields laid end to end.

A single thread of silk is stronger than the same size thread of some types of steel.

Glossary

antenna (More than one are called antennae.) long, skinny feeler on an insect's head

cocoon   silken case that protects the pupa inside it

domesticated   cared for by human beings

dye to change the color of fabric

hatch to come out of an egg

insect   small animal that has six legs, a body with three parts, and wings

larva   caterpillar-like stage of an insect's life when it eats and grows

mate   when a male and female come together to produce babies

moisture   water, wetness

moth   insect with a thick body and four broad wings. A moth is similar to a butterfly.

molt   shed the outer skin to allow an insect to grow

predator   animal that eats other animals

pupa   resting stage in an insect's life between larva and adult

raise   to care for an animal or plant until it is fully grown

scent   odor or smell

strand   thread or string

More Books to Read

Hartley, Karen, Chris Macro, and Philip Taylor. *Caterpillar.* Des Plaines, Ill.: Heinemann Library, 1999.

Legg, Gerald. *From Caterpillar to Butterfly.* Danbury, Conn.: Franklin Watts, 1998.

Schaffer, Donna. *Silkworms.* Mankato, Minn.: Capstone Press, 1999.

Index